Whispers of Sampaguita

A Memoir in Verses

SOPHIA JOELLE KHOTIL

ECHOWOVEN
PUBLISHING

First Edition: December 2025

ISBN: 979-8-218-87072-0

Printed in the United States of America

www.sophiajoellekhotil.com

@sophiajoelle_writer

For Mama and Papa

who built a home across oceans

and taught me that love can bloom

in any soil.

For Nanay and Daddy

whose memories and tenderness

continue to guide my steps

long after their voices have quieted.

And for every soul

who carries the scent of home

wherever they go.

Even oceans cannot drown the fragrance of home;
it lingers in the folds of language and dream.
Sampaguita — the flower of promise — reminds me
that what is lost can still return in bloom.

Table of Contents

Prologue

Before I learned the language of distance, I learned the language of flowers.

Not the roses in Western storybooks, nor the lilies arranged for holidays—but the wild, unassuming Sampaguita that seemed to bloom everywhere in the heat of the archipelago. I was born in Bacolod City, in a Philippines formerly labeled a third-world nation, where the air was thick with resilience and the scent of jasmine drifted through open windows like a quiet blessing. There, everything felt both fragile and enduring at once—much like the country itself, much like the people who raised me.

As a child, I didn't understand how something so small could carry so much meaning. I did not yet know that the Sampaguita was a promise, surviving sun, storms, and scarcity with a softness that refused to break. I only knew its fragrance followed us—clinging to hair, to the corners of worn suitcases, to the memory of a place we would eventually leave behind.

Years later, in a land that measured time differently— by seasons, by ambition, by cold mornings and crowded freeways—I began to hear it again. Soft at first. A breath behind a closed door. A whisper rising from a cup of tea; from a song I didn't know I remembered; from the way my mother said my name when she thought no one was listening.

This book is born from those whispers; from stories shaped by migration; from the ache of belonging to two worlds at once.

If you lean in—past the noise, past the years—you may hear it too.

A flower offering its truth: what is soft is not weak. What is small is not silent. And what survives does so with intention.

Here, in these pages, the Sampaguita speaks; I am finally ready to listen.

The Land That Promised Sky

I was four…
when my mother packed a suitcase full of sunlight,
and whispered —
Inday,[1]
we're going to the land
where dreams don't sleep.

I left behind family I loved,
a country I could barely remember,
for a life I had only known through Disney postcards
and Mickey Mouse ears.
Everything else —
America —
was waiting like a storybook
I wasn't sure I'd ever understand.

She whispered the promise of freedom into her kisses onto
my forehead —
soft,
gentle,
like something worth believing in.

---

[1] A Visayan term of endearment for a younger girl or sister.

America smiled

with white teeth

and wide flags.

She said, *Welcome.*

But her hands…

were already counting

how much we owed her

for the privilege of her streets.

In school,

I learned new alphabets

that erased the taste of *salamat* [2] from my tongue.

My teacher said I was lucky.

My classmates said I was different.

And I said nothing —

just traced the shape of my name

until it sounded like

a stranger

calling home.

Mama worked *one* job —

but that one job

was a thousand tiny sacrifices stitched together.

---

[2] *Thank you* in Tagalog

She took care of the elderly —
held hands that shook like paper,
wiped faces that forgot their own names,
fed strangers as gently
as she once fed me.

She cleaned rooms that smelled of medicine and time,
where every breath was a reminder
that love doesn't always live in family.

She came home smelling of a musty nursing facility and hope,
hours stolen
from my brother and me,
and still asked,
"Did you eat, Inday?"
Like love was a language
she could speak even through exhaustion.
Papa worked night shifts —
his hands always smelling of metal and grit.
He dreamed in fluorescent light
until one night…
the light stayed on,
and he didn't wake.

They said,

He's in a better place.

But I still look for him

in the hum of streetlamps,

in every quiet morning

Mama fills

with prayer.

Papa never got to see me

pledge my allegiance

on a Bible

the day I became a citizen —

the day I carried his dream

like a candle in both hands,

burning and heavy,

but mine to keep alive.

Mama told me,

"Study hard. Be better.

Make them see

you deserve to be here."

So, I built a tower of perfect grades —

each one

a brick of silence,

each one

heavier than the last.

I learned early

that freedom has borders

drawn in fear.

Freedom, they said,

was a flag

you could wrap yourself in.

But when I did,

it felt like a curtain —

something to hide

the brown of my skin,

something to muffle

the sea

still calling my name.

Now grown,

I walk beneath neon promises —

Land of opportunity.

Dream big.

Work hard.

But I know better.

Freedom here

is expensive —
and it charges interest
on every part of you
that doesn't fit its frame.

Still...
when I look up,
the sky is wide enough
to remember both names.
Maybe that's my freedom —
to stand here,
Filipina
and American,
awake inside a dream
that was never made for me...
and still —
I keep dreaming
anyway.

No Tuk Tuks in L.A.

I landed in a city of flat roads and endless lanes,
no *tuk tuks* [3] whirring, no jostling three-wheeled chaos.
Just cars that obey lights, engines humming polite,
not the dance of Bacolod City streets where horns and
laughter collide.

I remembered bright yellow, green, red
zipping past *sari-sari* [4] stores,
neighbors leaning out to greet,
vendors shouting over the engine's roar.

Here, everything was orderly, quiet,
and I missed the tilt, the squeak,
the small world of movement on tiny wheels
that carried my childhood in its bump and sway.

I longed for that mess of colors and sound,
for the city that smelled of gasoline, chicken *inasal* [5], and
durian,
for the ride that made you feel alive
because you never knew who would wave next.

---

[3] A motorbike with a passenger sidecar
[4] A corner family-run sundry or convenience store
[5] A Visayan grilled chicken with its distinctive flavors of sweet, sour and
aromatics

Somewhere Out There

Tito Chua sang with a voice
that cracked at the edges—
soft, trembling,
like it knew how to hold love and loss
in the same note.

When I was small,
he'd sing to me accompanied by the cicadas,
a radio humming low beside us,
the air thick with humidity and care.
He'd tap my nose,
call me his little listener,
and fill the afternoon
with songs that made even the dogs go quiet.

When I left for the States,
he sent me a cassette—
hand-labeled, the ink a little smudged—
and on it, his voice again,
singing *"Somewhere Out There."*

Halfway through,
you can hear him choke up,

a quiet sob caught in the tape hiss,

like a secret he didn't mean to send.

I played it over and over—

that small, trembling bridge between worlds,

his voice crossing the ocean

when I couldn't.

When I hear that song in passing,

I feel him there,

somewhere out there,

still singing through static,

still crying a little,

still loving me

from Heaven.

First Light at Disneyland

I stepped into the park—
cotton candy, churro carts,
laughter bouncing off every wall,
a half-eaten mouse popsicle
dripping on my tiny Payless shoes.

Colors spun past,
floats, fireworks, magic—
the teacup ride spinning me dizzy,
hands clutching the wheel,
heart spinning faster than the cups,
everything too big, too bright, too alive.

Then I heard it—
It's a Small World,
singing in a river of voices,
and somewhere in the melody,
Tagalog:
"Napakaliit talaga ng mundo,"
"Kay liit ng mundo na ito." [6]

---

[6] "It's a small world after all."

My chest tightened—
the song knew me,
the world knew me,
and for a moment,
I belonged.

I held my parents' hands tight,
anchors in a world
I was only just learning,
every ride a story,
every corner a universe
that smelled of sugar,
possibility,
and magic
that never left me.

Before He and She

In my first tongue,
there were no he or she—
just *siya* [7],
soft and whole,
like a shell cupped in your palm,
holding every kind of person.

No need to choose sides of a word,
no battle between boy and girl.
Everyone was simply *siya*,
as if language already knew
we were all made of the same breath.

Then came English,
with its sharp edges,
its labels like fences.
He. She.
Each one a box I had to fit people into,
each sentence a tiny correction
on the way I saw the world.

I stumbled through grammar
like learning to divide the ocean—

---

[7] They/them

to say who was which,

and what was what.

But sometimes,

in the quiet between thoughts,

siya still rises,

fluid and kind,

reminding me that in the language I first loved,

we were never meant

to be split apart by pronouns.

First Lessons

My first dose of cruelty came with a doll.
New country, new words stuck in my throat—
English tasted like marbles,
heavy and round, rolling the wrong way.

I just wanted to play.
The girls had dolls with shiny hair
and tiny shoes that clicked when they walked.
I held mine out, smiling,
hoping kindness sounded the same
in every language.

They laughed instead—
sharp and quick,
like scissors cutting a string.
I didn't understand the words,
but I understood *meantime*—
the space between my wanting
and their rejection.

Later, it was the boy—
the one with the BB gun,
his grin always one step ahead of mean.
He shot birds for fun,

14

left their small, broken bodies
on our doorstep like gifts.
Tiny wings still half open,
as if they were trying to fly away
from whatever made him that way.

Mama would sweep them into a bag,
whisper prayers I didn't know in English yet,
and tell me not to look.
But I always did.
Because something in me
needed to remember what cruelty looked like
before it had words.

Now, when I see children playing—
laughing without knowing
how language can wound—
I think of those dolls,
those birds,
and the small girl who learned too early
that silence isn't weakness—
it's survival
in a tongue not yet your own.

Ghost Tongue

I learned English
like chewing on chalk,
letters sharp in my mouth,
cutting the edges of the words I used to know.

Illonggo [8]—my first heartbeat,
my Nanay's voice in the kitchen,
the stories our housemaids whispered
between mango trees and the river
by our tin roof house—
slipping, sliding,
leaving me hollow.

At school, they laughed at my accent,
so I swallowed my Mama's words,
let them fall away
like leaves in a dry season.

Now, I open my mouth
and Illonggo hides,
a ghost in the corners of my teeth,
a song I almost remember,

[8] The Hiligaynon language spoken in the Visayas region of the Philippines

but the chorus is gone,

and I am still trying to sing it.

Golden Afternoons in Altadena Dr.

The sun sneaks in like a shy visitor,
gold dust spilling across the carpet,
catching in the hair at my forehead,
warming the backs of my legs as I lie on the couch.

From somewhere close, somewhere just out of reach,
mariachi music blares—
trumpets and violins laughing,
a neighbor's party drifting through the walls,
filling our quiet apartment with rhythm I cannot touch.

I hear the ice cream truck,
its tinny jingle rolling slowly down the street,
and I imagine the Pink Panther popsicle
waiting for me, cold and pink and sweet,
a tiny prize for surviving the heat,
the music, the long, lazy stretch of afternoon.

Somewhere far away, kids in the Philippines
still wash clothes in the river,
water rippling around their knees,
feet bare on the stones,
and walk dirt roads in oversized flip flops

just to get candy from the corner *tindahan* [9],
smiles bright under the same golden sun.

What a difference—my life here in the U.S.,
plush floors, ice cream trucks, sun sneaking through
windows,
a soft couch instead of river stones,
my candy waiting instead of earned in dirt and heat.

Time moves softly here,
slowed by sunlight,
by the hum of life outside,
by sticky fingers and sticky floors,
by the way a day like this
seems to stretch forever,
just so I can taste it,
remember it,
and fold it into myself.

---

[9] Market

New Holidays

Back home,
the calendar smelled of fiestas—
processions, *Masskara* [10] parades,
rosaries whispered through candle smoke.
But in America,
the months came dressed in glitter and glue.

At school, I learned new magic:
cutting paper clovers,
searching the grass for one with four leaves,
as if luck could grow just anywhere.
Then November came
with paper plates turned turkeys,
glued feathers fanning out in every color
while teachers spoke of pilgrims and thanks—
words that felt strange
but sweet on my tongue.

And October—
oh, October—
when we dressed as witches and superheroes,
faces sticky with candy and awe.

---

[10] A colorful festival celebrating the resilience of the people of Bacolod
City with masks and floats

We knocked on strangers' doors

and they gave us sugar

just for pretending.

It felt like a secret I was finally allowed to keep.

Each holiday was a new word

in the language of belonging,

and though I didn't always understand the stories,

I learned joy in translation—

how even in a foreign season,

a child can find wonder

in paper, glue, and the taste of something new.

Two Breakfasts

In the Philippines,
morning came soft and savory—
steam rising from rice like breath,
fried fish crisping in the pan,
the air alive with vinegar and salt.
Mama slicing papaya,
their golden cheeks glistening in the sun,
pickled radish sharp and sweet on the tongue.
Breakfast was a full story there—
a memory served warm,
a promise that the day had already begun.

Here, in America,
morning comes in boxes—
cartoons on cardboard,
frosted flakes that promise happiness
if you add enough sugar.
Sausages spitting in the skillet,
pancakes stacked like clouds,
syrup pooling where the ocean used to be.

It's sweet, yes—
but too sweet.
Like it's trying to cover something missing.

No fish bones to pick clean,

no papaya juice dripping down my wrist,

no chatter spilling out from an open window.

Sometimes I pour the cereal,

watch the milk rise like a quiet tide,

and think of home—

of papayas and rice,

of mornings that tasted like salt and sun,

of how even breakfast

knew where it came from.

Green Mangoes and Ginamos

We sat on the cracked steps,
plastic plate between us,
a green mango sliced like sunshine
that wasn't ready yet.

The air smelled of sweat and afternoon—
dust, sea salt, and *ginamos* [11]—
that stinky, sacred paste
Nanay kept in an old ice cream tub.

We dipped each slice deep,
wrinkling our noses first,
then biting,
eyes squinting from the shock—
the sour, the salt, the sting—
and laughing like we'd done something bad.

Neighbors passed,
pretending not to judge,
but we saw their mouths water too.

Nothing else tasted like home—
not candy, not cake—

---

[11] Fermented fish or shrimp paste

just that green bite,

that dirty joy,

and the smell that clung to our fingers

long after the sun went down.

Change

Mama pushes the cart down the fluorescent aisle,
quarters clinking like tiny reminders of work.
She dumps a mountain of clothes into a drum,
pours in detergent measured in neat plastic caps,
and presses buttons that whirl, tumble, and spin
without a whisper of river stones or sunshine.

Her hands move over the wet fabric—
but not with mud-stained patience
or the slow rhythm of rinsing in the river behind our old
house.
Here, it's clean and quick,
no laughter of cousins echoing,
no breeze teasing the wet strands of hair,
just hums and clicks,
and Mama, quietly folding
the world into neat, dry piles.

I watch her work
and remember the river—
how water carried soap suds downstream
and held the sun on its back.
Now the laundromat hums,
and Mama hums too,

but the song feels smaller

than the river that once sang to her hands.

Toto

I remember the hush before they brought *Toto* [12] home—
the way the house seemed to hold its breath,
my toys lined up like witnesses
to the end of an era.

The first American citizen in our family.
How drastic our two worlds were—
I grew up bathing with a hand pump, typically used in third-
world nations.
He would grow up bathing in an enamel-coated sink.

Eight years old,
I already knew how to be the center—
how to draw laughter like sunlight,
how to earn the extra scoop of ice cream.

Then suddenly,
everyone's voice bent softly toward a cradle.
He was small—
so small I thought he might disappear
if I blinked too long.

---

[12] A term of endearment for a young boy or younger brother

Wrapped in cotton clouds,

he made even the air move quieter.

Visitors came and said things like,

"He looks just like your Papa,"

"He's so handsome,"

"Poor Inday, she's not the baby anymore."

And I smiled,

the kind of smile that hides behind its teeth,

while my heart tried to learn

how to make space.

I got promoted from *Inday* to *Manang* [13].

But later—

when the house emptied,

and Mama handed him to me—

he opened his eyes,

and they were so wide, so sure,

like he already knew me.

His tiny hand curled around my finger

and something inside me shifted—

not broken, not gone,

just stretched into something bigger.

---

[13] A term of endearment for an older girl or sister

I realized then:

I wasn't losing the light,

just learning

how to share it.

Crayons in the Canyon

The crayons melted first—
a waxy rainbow bleeding into the cup holder
of our old Nissan sedan.
The windows hummed with heat,
and I pressed my forehead to the glass
just to feel the road move.

Papa said we were almost there,
and I believed him—
because he always said that,
and because the ride itself was half the magic.
Snack wrappers rustled like lullabies,
and the air conditioner coughed
its tired, dusty breath.

Then the world opened—
so wide, so endless
that my breath caught somewhere in my chest.
The Grand Canyon.
Bigger than anything I could have drawn
with those crayons now melted into color puddles.
The sky seemed to lean down and look with us,
like it, too, couldn't believe its own reflection.

Somewhere in all that wonder,

I got a nosebleed—

thin red lines down my arm,

as if my body couldn't hold

that much beauty inside.

Mama pressed a tissue to my face,

half worried, half laughing,

saying, *"Even your blood's dramatic."*

And I laughed,

because she was right.

The road always did that to me—

made me feel bigger and smaller at once,

safe in the thrum of the tires,

the soft rattle of maps in the glovebox,

the smell of melted crayons,

gasoline and dreams.

Now, whenever I drive,

and the horizon stretches too far to measure,

I think of that canyon—

how the earth cracked open

to show us its heart,

and how I learned, somewhere between

a nosebleed and a wax puddle,

the road,

somehow,

always felt like home.

Lumpia and Love

Family parties—
I still hear them sometimes,
in the quiet bustle of my own kitchen.

That echo of laughter,
that off-key karaoke that somehow
sounded like home.

I remember being small,
the air thick with oil and joy,
lumpia [14] sizzling like it was telling secrets
only the hungry could understand.

Someone always singing from the soul,
even when the mic crackled,
even when the lyrics were half-forgotten—
because the heart remembered everything.

I miss that.

---

[14] A Filipino spring roll

The crowd of *titas* [15] in floral blouses,

their bangles clinking like tiny applause.

The *titos* [16] teasing, the kids darting

between legs sticky with soda and freedom.

Mahjongg tiles clattering across tables,

sharp little rhythms under the hum of voices,

plastic plates bending under

too much food and too much love.

Now the nights are quieter.

No voices spilling out the doorway,

no rice cooker chorus in the background.

And sometimes I ache

for that heat, that noise, that us—

for the sound of being known,

for the kind of love

that smelled like garlic and home.

---

[15] Aunts

[16] Uncles

Terracotta Pots

My third birthday—
the whole *barangay* [17] came.
Kids running wild through the courtyard,
dust kicking up like laughter,
like joy had feet.

We didn't have a piñata—
no paper donkey swinging from a tree,
just terracotta pots,
lined up like tiny treasures,
bellies full of candy,
waiting to be tipped,
or cracked open by large sticks.

Mama made the food look like a dream—
rainbow marshmallows on skewers,
soft and glowing under the afternoon light,
sweet spaghetti tangled with hotdogs,
sauce so red it looked like celebration.
Paper plates bending under the weight of joy,
and someone's *tito* singing off-key to the radio—

---

[17] Neighborhood

because in the *baranggay*,

every song sounds better when you mean it.

Then the first pot broke—

crack!

and the world exploded into sugar.

Kids dove,

hands flying,

pockets swelling with sweetness.

I just stood there—

grinning with icing on my cheek,

like I owned the sun for a second.

I was three,

and that little yard

was the whole universe.

No one talked about bills,

or borders,

or the years that would scatter us.

Just candy,

and laughter,

and Mama's tired, happy smile

shining like it could hold time still.

Now, every time I see a terracotta pot,

I remember—

how joy once came so easy,

how love once fit

inside a cracked pot

and a handful of sweets,

shared with everyone

who showed up.

Feathers and Fury

The sun hangs low,

dust swirling in the yard,

somewhere nearby,

roosters squared off,

feathers gleaming, heat bouncing off the ground.

We don't see the fight—

just hear it:

crowing, clatter,

men shouting, leaning over fences,

coins jingling,

adrenaline slicing the afternoon air.

I press my face to the open door,

tiny hands gripping the frame,

heart pounding with the rhythm of wings and yells,

and I feel bad for the roosters—

small bodies forced to fight,

bright eyes wild,

caught in a game I don't understand.

I can still remember the tension,

the thrill,

the shame,

the smell of earth, sweat, feathers

hanging heavy

long after the roosters went home.

Coffee Table Picnic

It was just salad and pasta—
nothing fancy,
just lettuce slick with bottled dressing
and noodles soft from the boil.
But Mama called me to the living room
like it was a feast.

She spread out two plates
on the coffee table,
poured juice into mismatched glasses,
and said, *"Come on, Inday,
let's eat here tonight."*

So we sat cross-legged on the carpet,
the TV light flickering like candles,
and it felt like a celebration—
our own secret holiday.
No aunts shouting in the kitchen,
no cousins grabbing the last piece of fried fish,
no clatter of ten spoons on melamine plates.
Just her and me,
and the buzz of the refrigerator
in our quiet apartment.

Coming to America
was supposed to mean more—
more space, more comfort, more future—
but the silence after dinner
was loud enough to fill a house.

Still, Mama smiled,
twirled her fork like we were dining fine,
and said, *"See? We can still make it nice."*
And she did.
Every bite tasted like trying,
like making do,
like love in translation.

Now, when I eat at a coffee table,
no matter how grown I am,
I remember that night—
how she turned a small meal
into a memory big enough
to keep us from feeling alone.

Through Rabbit Ears

Our TV was tiny, perched on a wooden stand,
rabbit ears crooked, hunting signals in the air.
No Sesame Street, no Bluey,
just the flashing world of crime and chases,
where Fred Dryer stomped through city streets,
gun in hand, justice in his stride.

Explosions bounced off the walls,
my heart thumped in rhythm with sirens,
my small fingers pressed to the screen,
learning Western civilization
through detective shows, car crashes, and smoke.

On quiet nights, Rambo carved a path of fury,
while The Sound of Music sang me into dreams
of mountains and sunlight,
of something soft, something tender,
between all the gunfire and grit.

I grew up on fragments, on bursts of sound and color,
on heroes who saved the day before bedtime,
and in that small box with crooked antennas,
I glimpsed a world larger than my living room,

and held it like a secret treasure,

all explosions and lullabies tangled together.

Piss Pot

I slept beneath mosquito netting,
its lace halo draped from the ceiling,
turning my bed into a small white world
where the hum of wings sang me to sleep.

Beside me—a piss pot,
chipped and humble,
waiting like an old friend
for midnight's quiet emergencies.

It smelled faintly of soap and rust,
a secret we didn't talk about.

Some nights, I'd imagine the children in America—
rooms painted soft pastels,
night-lights shaped like stars,
toilets that flushed with a button's grace,
no need for nets,
no buzzing lullabies,
no tin roof dripping onto dreams.

Still, I loved the sound of rain
tapping against our world of woven screens,

Nanay's voice floating in from the other room,
the smell of rice left to keep warm.

I didn't know it then,
but that piss pot and that net
held more safety than porcelain ever could—
a small, imperfect comfort
under a roof that kept
both mosquitoes and the world at bay.

Daddy, Hunter, and the Pig

Morning smells like earth,
straw, wet fur, life—alive, breathing.

Daddy grips the spear,
hands steady,
the same hands that held me,
that held our family,
now moving with quiet authority.

Hunter circles, tail wagging, alert,
nose twitching,
like he knows this is a dance
we've done a thousand times before.

I watch—small, wide-eyed—
each thrust precise, deliberate,
Daddy teaching without words
what care looks like,
what survival feels like.

Hunter barks, or maybe just reminds us:
life goes on.
Even endings have purpose.

And I learn,

early,

memory is stitched from smells,

sounds, hands,

and the creatures

who walk beside us.

A Pair of Latchkey Kids

We met like the world had been waiting—
two latchkey kids
with keys on strings around our necks
and too much time between the last bell and sunset.

Marcy lived across the apartment plaza in the Castilian,
past the laundry room,
where dryers rattled like background music,
and the soda machine hummed like a secret.

That plaza was our playground,
our world between worlds—
the place where grown-ups weren't watching
and we could be anything.

The year she got chicken pox,
we became healers,
witches, scientists—
gathering juniper and cypress sprigs
from around her apartment.
We crushed them in our hands,
made a bath that smelled like green fire,
and swore it would cure her itching.

And somehow,

I think it did—

or maybe it was just the magic of being believed in.

We ate spaghetti the way only kids could—

spaghetti sauce swirled with sour cream.

I was also witness to how she melded El Salvador

in an American dinner staple

and somehow, I didn't feel alone anymore.

We shared food like secrets:

she introduced me to pupusas,

warm, golden, the way they make them in her country—

and I introduced her to *Dinuguan* [18],

told her it was chocolate soup.

She tried it,

made a face,

and then found out the truth—

and her nose wrinkled,

her eyes wide,

totally grossed out,

because some truths hit harder than laughter.

And we weren't always safe in our little world—

---

[18] A Filipino delicacy made of pork offal and simmered in a dark gravy of pig's blood, garlic and peppers

we had seen it, too:

the day they wheeled a young woman down the plaza,

covered in a tarp,

after some terrible, unthinkable thing.

Homicide,

and the grown-ups whispered,

but we just stared,

hearts hammering,

eyes wide open,

knowing the world could be bigger and darker than we'd ever

imagined.

And at school—

we got caught lying.

Something dumb,

something that started as a joke

and grew teeth.

Our teacher sat us down,

looked us right in the eyes,

and said,

"Have you heard The Boy Who Cried Wolf?"

And we nodded,

trying to look sorry,

trying not to smile.

Because we knew the story,

but we also knew
we'd tell a thousand more.

That was us—
bold, barefoot,
too loud for the hallway,
too curious for the rules.
Two girls making myths out of ordinary afternoons.

And sometimes now,
when the world feels too big,
I still smell juniper,
taste pupusas and can't eat spaghetti without sour cream,
feel the sting of sun on concrete,
hear her laugh—or her disgust—
bouncing off the plaza walls—
and I know
childhood never really leaves.

It just hides in the corners of my heart,
still laughing softly,
like Marcy.

Desert Stops

We were always somewhere between here and there—
Mama in the passenger seat,
Papa humming to the radio,
the air thick with the smell of gas station coffee
and sunscreen melting on my skin.

The road stretched like a ribbon,
fading into heat waves and mirages,
and somewhere in the middle of nowhere
Papa would slow down,
pull over,
and say, "*Let's stretch our legs.*"

We'd tumble out—
the wind dry and endless,
our shadows long and wavering.
There'd be a little roadside shop,
selling rocks, postcards, and dreamcatchers.
Mama would let me choose one thing—
a shiny stone,
a scorpion keychain,
a snow globe with no snow.
Tiny treasures that smelled like dust and freedom.

The desert was empty,
but it never felt lonely.
Colors glowed differently there—
orange like heat,
blue like silence,
and pink like the sky holding its breath at dusk.

When night came,
Papa would park the car
and we'd step out into the melody of crickets and wind.
The stars were so many,
so close,
I thought I could scoop them up
and keep one in my pocket.

Those road trips taught me
how vast this new world really was—
how far the sky could stretch,
how small I could feel
and still belong.
That beauty hides
in rest stops and rattling air vents,
and love sounds like
laughter on an endless road
beneath a sky that never ends.

Ducks and Fever

I was under four—
small enough to disappear in a hug,
big enough to see ducks
marching across the road.

"Tita Judith!" I shouted,
my words tumbling like stones—
"look! The ducks—they're crossing!"

Then everything shook—
my body a drum I couldn't control,
hot fire pulsing through me,
the room spinning like those tiny ducks
waddling, fearless, crossing.

They put me in a tub of ice—
water biting, shocking, sharp,
cold wrapping around me
like it could take the fever away.

Tita Judith's hands—
anchors, gentle, soft,

pulling me back

from a world I didn't know I was leaving.

And even now,

I remember the ducks,

the tremor, the ice, the fear,

and how love

could hold a little body

when I couldn't hold myself.

Nanay's Garden

Air thick with green—
hibiscus, bougainvillea,
plumeria petals sharp and sweet
after a monsoon rain.

Ferns curl like secrets,
palms sway like they're listening.

Nanay [19] moves between them,
hands wet with soil,
hands full of love,
whispering to ginger,
to orchids,
to trembling dragonfruit seedlings
that soak up the sun.

Cicadas sing.
Breeze carries rain stories.

---

[19] My paternal grandmother

Mornings spent barefoot,
laughter climbing like vines
around every stem.

I close my eyes now—
and I'm there,
smelling her garden,
living in its bloom.

Chosen Family

I grew up surrounded by *Titos* and *Titas*—
not of my blood,
but of my life,
their laughter spilling into our tiny living room
like sunlight through slatted windows.

Tita Emma with her endless stories,
Tito Nelson who smelled like cigarettes and cheap cologne,
each one folding me into their world
as if I had always belonged.

At birthdays, fiestas, random Tuesdays,
their hugs were as natural as Nanay's,
their voices as warm as home.

I never counted them—
didn't need to.
In that messy, beautiful village,
blood was only one thread among many.

And now, whenever I see a familiar face,
or hear a laugh that feels like sunlight,
I remember: family is chosen,
and love doesn't ask for a last name.

Bear Claw

He was jogging just ahead of us,
steady breaths, the slap of sneakers
keeping time with the morning.
Mama and I were walking to her job—
her purse bouncing against her hip,
my hand small and sure in hers.

Then he slowed.
Then he swayed.
Then—
he was on the ground,
a sound like air leaving the world.

Mama screamed for help,
her voice sharper than the sirens that hadn't come yet.
I remember the stillness of him—
the way his chest didn't move,
the thin line of blood
trickling from the corner of his mouth
and pooling into the cracks of the sidewalk.

Someone ran for a phone.
Someone shouted directions.

And then—
the donut shop.

The bell chimed as we stepped inside,
the warm smell of sugar
suffocating the morning.
The cashier took one look at me,
then at Mama,
and said softly,
"She shouldn't see this."

Mama's breath was ragged
as the woman handed me a Bear Claw—
warm, sticky, sweet.
I held it like something holy,
watched the glaze melt
and run between my fingers.

Outside, life had stopped.
Inside, I chewed and swallowed
because I didn't know what else to do.

And even now,
when I taste pastry sugar on my tongue,
I remember that morning—
the man who never got up,

and how Mama's hand trembled

when she reached for mine again.

Sundays at Pearson's Port

Sunlight bounced off the marina waves,
I clutched a pail, tiny fingers chasing shells
across the wobbly deck,
while the smell of salt and fish
mingled with the whir of hungry shoppers inside.

Snapper glistened on ice,
shrimp curled like small moons,
each one a promise of dinner
waiting for our hands to bring them home.

Daddy's sea snails were different—
plucked from brackish water, still wiggling—
but this was close enough,
a taste of the sea I could hold in my own palms.

We'd rush back, salivating across the dock,
broil the fish until it smelled like fire and ocean,
or let the shrimp melt into a steaming soup,
our Sunday night laughter rising with the steam.

Even now, I can feel that deck sway,
hear the water lapping against the hull,
taste the salt on my lips,

and know that some Sundays

never truly leave us.

Salt and Shells

I ran to the sea—
naked.
Everyone else—clothed, restrained,

I—skin bare to the sun,
to the wind,
to the waves that called my name.

Daddy [20] waded in,
hands slick with salt,
grabbing sea snails off rocks,
clinging, stubborn, alive.

We ate them—raw, briny, strange,
tongues tasting the ocean itself,
laughter spilling over the tide,
sand sticking to shoulders,
water tangling hair,
and I felt infinite.

---

[20] My paternal grandfather

A child of salt,

of sun,

of Daddy's hands,

of freedom

before the world could say no.

Holy Eucharist with Sprinkles

I wore white lace,
a veil soft as whispers,
floating over my small shoulders.
St. Cecilia's pews smelled of polished wood
and candle smoke,
and I knelt—hands folded,
heart murmuring prayers I barely understood.

Sunday school came after—
donuts, sprinkles and sugar dusted over fingers,
punch in wax paper cups
dribbling down my wrist
like tiny celebrations I didn't have to earn.

Even when we moved countries,
Mama and Papa found prayer
in whispered Masses,
in the laughter of neighbors,
in communities stitched together
with hope and faith,
even far from home.

And I remember—
the shimmer of my dress,

the echo of hymns,

the sweetness of belonging,

of family, of God,

of love carried across oceans,

sticky fingers and all.

The Talking Bird

We had a talking Mynah bird—
black feathers slick as oil,
eyes sharp with mischief,
perched near the kitchen window
where gossip and garlic floated all day.

Every morning it called out,
"Maayong aga!" [21] bright as sunlight,
as if blessing the house awake.
But before we could smile back,
it would cackle, tilt its head,
and shout something foul
about someone's crotch.
Our maids would howl with laughter,
covering their mouths too late.

The bird learned fast—
faster than prayer,
faster than discipline—
and so did I.

---

[21] Good morning!

Soon I was echoing its wicked songs,
the house filled with mayhem and giggles,
Nanay's slippers slapping the floor
as she chased us both into silence.

But oh, how alive those mornings were—
the sun, the laughter, the forbidden words
fluttering like feathers in the air.

To this day, when I hear a bird greet the dawn,
I almost expect it to curse,
and for a second,
I miss that small, foul-mouthed friend
who taught me the music
of mischief and language all at once.

Air Shows

Papa would wake me early,
the sun barely stretching its arms,
and say, *"Get ready, Inday—*
we're going to the air show."

He'd wear his aviator glasses,
the kind that caught the whole sky in their reflection,
and Mama, always stylish,
with her perm and her white visor,
looked like she belonged in a postcard
from another decade.

We'd park in a sea of cars
on dry grass that crunched under our shoes.
The smell of jet fuel and popcorn
mingled in the wind—
sharp, exciting,
like the air itself was buzzing with engines.

He lifted me onto his shoulders,
his hands firm around my legs,
and from up there
the world stretched wide and endless—
planes roaring like thunder,

trails of smoke looping through the blue,
my heart racing with every dive and twist.

Then came the thunder—
jets slicing the sky,
leaving trails of smoke like chalk lines
drawn by the gods.
I'd cover my ears and laugh,
feeling the sound in my ribs,
the kind of thrill you don't outgrow.

Papa's glasses flashed
with every loop and dive,
and Mama clapped with both hands,
her visor barely holding back the wind.

Those days smelled like sunscreen and pride,
like family and flight—
and even now,
when I hear a jet tear through the sky,
I see them—
Papa, steady in his shades,
Mama radiant in the sun,
and me between them,
eyes to the sky,
believing we could all take off too.

White Grain

I tried to walk away—
to peel myself from sticky bowls
and steaming baskets,
to forget the smell of night-market rice
mingling with *Datu Puti, Mang Tomas* [22], and garlic.

In America, I reached for bread,
toast, bagels, cereal—
things that didn't weigh me down
with history I wasn't ready to carry.
I wanted to be unmoored,
to be light.

But rice finds a way.
It curls into my dreams,
sticking to my fingers like memory,
sitting beside every family gathering I avoided,
laughing in the sizzle of lumpia,
the peace of Nanay's kitchen.

I love it.
I hate it.
It is comfort, burden, identity, rebellion.

---

[22] Traditional Filipino condiments

Each grain a story I once denied,

now impossible to untangle

from the parts of me I thought I could leave behind.

Even when I try to ignore it, the steam rises,

and I am pulled back, home again.

Half-Understood

I'm in the middle of the grocery aisle,
or maybe the post office,
or the library where silence is supposed to live—
and someone sees me.

A Filipino face lights up,
and suddenly Tagalog spills out—
words rolling fast,
smiling eyes,
the warmth of home I almost remember.

I nod.
I smile.
My brain scrambles
for syllables I know,
but they're ghosts.
They slip.
I catch nothing.

"I... I don't understand," I say,
and suddenly their eyes widen,
hands waving,
gestures tumbling,
smiles softening into patience.

They scramble to connect,

mixing English, pointing, laughing,

trying to bridge the gap

between our shared skin and my silent confusion.

I laugh too late, or too little,

feeling the ache of wanting

to be at home,

but not quite knowing how.

And when they finally leave,

I carry the memory like a whisper—

of warmth,

of effort,

of a language almost mine.

Halo-Halo

A cup of chaos, carefully layered—
shaved ice like frozen sunlight,
condensed milk drizzling down
like a quiet surrender.

Red beans, kidney and mung,
sweetened like memory,
jackfruit ribbons curling
around the edges of my spoon.
Purple ube ice cream
perched on top like pride itself,
bold, unapologetic, impossible to ignore.

I stir it and it becomes a swirl—
every flavor colliding,
each texture speaking a different language,
but together, perfect.

This is me,
Filipina-American,
my identity a cup of contradictions:
rooted in scorched soil,
blended with sugar and rain,
layered over ice that chills but preserves,

flavors mingling,

strange and beautiful to those who do not know.

Every bite is a negotiation,

sweet, nutty, creamy, icy,

a reminder that we can exist

in the middle,

neither fully one thing nor the other,

and still be delicious,

still be whole.

Halo-halo [23]—

a mouthful of memory,

a celebration in a cup,

a reminder that blending does not dilute,

it deepens.

---

[23] A Filipino shaved ice dessert with milk, beans, fruits, jellies and ube ice cream

Thrill of the Unknown

He arrived with suitcases full of sun,
of Guitar Magazines and memories
he carried across oceans,
a teenager just learning
how wide this new world could be.

I took him to Disneyland,
hands sticky with kettle corn and soda,
smiles bouncing off every castle tower.
This, I said,
is America.

My cousin's eyes went wide at the spinning teacups,
at the pirates sailing in endless water,
but I had one plan:
Space Mountain—
the indoor rollercoaster,
all darkness and lasers,
a galaxy spinning just for us.

He stepped into the ride,
heart hammering like fireworks,
arms pressed tight against his chest.
And then—

we shot forward,

twisting, turning,

screams colliding with the hum of neon stars.

I watched him flail,

eyes squeezed shut,

face pale under the starlight,

and laughed and laughed

because this was my gift:

a "Welcome to America"

wrapped in darkness and light,

a first taste of thrill,

of fear,

of freedom.

When we got off,

he was shaking,

breath coming in quick, broken bursts,

but he smiled,

the kind of grin

that knew he had survived

something enormous,

something new,

and he would never forget

that first ride in the strange, bright land

he now calls home.

Lolo Agripino's Pear Tree

Lolo Agri [24] planted it years before I arrived—
a small pear tree in the backyard,
thin and trembling in the foreign wind.
He said it would grow strong,
just like us,
if we gave it time.

For years it was only leaves,
branches reaching but never giving,
until one summer afternoon
I saw the first fruit—
small, green, stubbornly alive.
Lolo plucked it,
wiped it on his sleeve,
and handed it to me
like an offering.

I bit in—
crisp, cold,
a shock of sweetness
I'd never known before.
Nothing like the mangoes of home,

---

[24] My maternal grandfather

soft and golden and dripping down your chin.

This was sharper, cleaner,

like tasting a new country.

Lolo smiled,

his eyes proud and a little sad.

He said, *"See? Sweetness grows here too."*

And I nodded,

juice running down my wrist,

not sure if he meant the tree,

or us.

Now it still stands,

its branches heavy with green memory.

Every fall, I remember that first taste—

how strange it was,

how beautiful,

how Lolo taught me

that even far from home,

we can still bear fruit.

River Rules

I was four—
thinking four meant brave,
thinking four meant ready—
ready to conquer the river
all by myself.

I grabbed a friend,
tiny hands clutching mine,
we marched like explorers,
barefoot with pebbles between toes,
sun hot on our backs,
hearts bigger than our bodies.

Nanay was looking for us—
her voice slicing the air
when she finally found us,
sharp as the river's edge,
hands gentle,
pulling us back
from the water we weren't ready for.

We protested, we argued,
but we listened—

because Nanay's rules
were love wrapped in warnings,
discipline that smelled of soap
and the river after rain.

I can still remember the thrill of thinking I was older,
the sting of being told no,
and the warmth of her arms
pulling me home.

Chiffon in South Texas

Tita Thelma cracked eggs like secrets,
measured sugar by feel,
whispered recipes in a mix of Ilonggo and love.
The oven hummed in that South Texas heat,
but she didn't mind—
said sweetness was worth the sweat.

I watched her fold the batter,
gentle as prayer,
the scent of vanilla
floating through her small kitchen
like a promise of home.

She called it *chiffon cake*,
light as laughter,
soft enough to make the heat outside disappear.
When it rose, golden and trembling,
she'd smile and say,
"Even here,
we can make something beautiful from scratch."

I learned more than baking—
I learned survival disguised as dessert,
how to find softness in a hard place,

how a slice of cake could hold

the whole sweetness of where we came from.

Townsfolk of La Castellana

Papa wore pride like a barong that never wrinkled—
President of Townsfolk of La Castellana,
his name printed bold on programs
that smelled of fresh ink and promise.

Those were our golden years.
The community wasn't just people—
it was family.
Laughter stitched into potlucks and raffles,
Ilonggo and English mingling like cousins
at long tables lined with foil trays
and paper flowers.

Then came the grand balls—
hotels with chandeliers that caught our awe,
tables draped in linen
too white to touch.
Mama in sequins,
Papa shaking hands like a statesman.
And me—
tiny, overdressed,
hair shellacked into place with too much hairspray,
dress shedding glitter like a trail of stardust
everywhere I went.

I'd run between tables,

nylon stockings slipping at the knees,

heels clicking on marble floors,

while grown-ups toasted to good work,

to hometowns remembered,

to bridges built across oceans.

Papa would look out at everyone—

the music swelling,

the laughter spilling past the walls—

and smile that smile

that said *we did this.*

We built something

out of distance and longing.

Now, when I see glitter on old photo albums,

or hear a ballroom song from that decade,

I think of those nights—

the soft clink of glasses,

the glow on Papa's face,

and how, for a while,

we were royalty of our own making,

a kingdom of homesick hearts

that found each other again

under hotel lights.

Green Treasure

In our rickety house,
where the floorboards sighed underfoot
and the windows rattled with the wind,
Nanay kept a little aquarium—
glass walls holding a tiny green world.

She tended it like a secret garden,
hands dipped carefully into the water,
lifting strands of seaweed
that swayed like quiet dancers.
The smell of salt and life
hung soft in the air.

When she offered it to me,
I hesitated—
this green, slippery treasure
so small in her hands,
so alive.

But she smiled, warm and certain,
and I tasted it,
and the ocean itself seemed to vibrate
inside my mouth.

It was delicious—

a memory of tides and sun and patience,

of her hands teaching me

that even in a rickety house

you could grow something extraordinary.

Stories That Stayed

In Weslaco, TX the air was thick—
manure from fields drifting through the dusk,
heat rising from the cracked earth
like something alive.

My cousins would whisper under the slow ceiling fan,
voices low, trembling between laughter and fear.

They spoke of the *manananggal*[25],
her wings slicing the moonlight in half,
of the *kapre*[26] smoking in the trees
where the streetlights never reached.
They said *duwende*[27] lived in the yard,
so we never kicked the mounds of earth—
we greeted them and said *"Tabi-tabi po,"*[28] just in case.

At night, the crickets fell silent,
and every rustle felt like a warning,
like the world holding its breath.

---

[25] A grotesque winged creature that detaches its torso from its lower half
and haunts at night
[26] A large, mythical, hairy creature that sits in trees and smokes cigars
[27] Small gnomes or dwarves that reside in trees and ant hills or mounds
[28] *Excuse me, please.*

I'd lie awake, eyes wide,

feeling the stories breathe around me—

half real, half remembered.

Now, years away from that house,

I still pause before dark windows,

still whisper apologies to unseen things.

Those tales—they never left.

They cling to me softly,

like the scent of Pancit on my clothes,

like home,

like magic I'm too old to believe—

and too Filipino to forget.

Snow of the Century

Every December,
Tita Mina's and Tito Eddie's house came alive—
a lantern glowing at the gate,
the scent of *lechon* [29] drifting down the street,
voices spilling out before the door even opened.

Inside, it was chaos in the best way:
karaoke blaring,
someone always off-key but proud of it,
Titos clapping,
Titas laughing so loud
you couldn't hear yourself think.

The table was a crown of food—
lechon glistening at the center,
pancit curling beside it,
bibingka steaming,
and bottles clinking like bells.
Someone always shouted *"Kaon ta!"* [30]
even though we'd already started.

---

[29] A whole roasted pig
[30] *Let's eat!*

My cousins and I stayed up all night—

sneaking soda and beer,

taking turns at karaoke,

pretending the night would never end.

The air smelled of roasted meat and joy,

and the laughter felt endless,

like the world was full and safe

and ours.

Then one Christmas Eve,

the impossible happened—

it snowed in tropical South Texas.

Flakes like whispers fell on palm leaves,

on corn stalks,

on our open mouths and astonished eyes.

They said it hadn't snowed in a hundred years.

For one night,

even the sky celebrated with us.

But years passed.

Tita Mina and Tito Eddie grew quiet,

and then they were gone.

The house stands still now—

windows clouded,

door rusted shut,

as if holding its breath.

Yet I swear,

if you walk by on a cold December night,

you can still hear it—

the echo of a love song off-key,

the clatter of plates,

the Baloco sisters' laughter rising like smoke.

All those memories,

still alive inside those walls,

still feasting,

still singing,

still calling us home.

Folding the Edges

Flour dust—
floating in the air like soft memories.
It lands on the counter,
on Mama's hands,
on mine—
and Tita's voice hums somewhere between laughter and a
song from the radio.

We're making *empanadas* [31] from scratch.
No store-bought shortcuts here,
just stories kneaded into dough.
Ground beef, sweet raisins,
green peas like tiny suns—
it smells like Sunday,
like everyone showed up hungry
and happy to be here.

Mama says, *"Press, fold, twist."*
Tita says, *"No, like this—*
you have to make the edges smile."
I try,
but mine come out lopsided,

---

[31] A savory pastry filled with beef, raisins, potatoes, peas and carrots

uneven,

a little too full of everything.

And they laugh—

that full, round, heart-sound kind of laugh—

and say,

"Pretty doesn't matter

if it tastes like love."

Oil starts snapping in the pan—

gold rising,

the smell filling every corner of the kitchen

like we're sealing in the past.

We talk over each other,

switching between English and Ilonggo,

the words themselves seasoned

with affection and heat.

Someone tells a story about a cousin,

someone else swats at the smoke,

and we taste one too early—

burn our tongues—

but none of us stop smiling.

Because this—

this is what home tastes like:

hot crust,

sweet salt,

a little burn on your lips,

and the sound of women you love

turning ordinary afternoons

into something worth remembering.

And when the last empanada cools,

and the laughter fades into quiet,

I swear I can still feel it—

their joy folded into every edge,

their hands guiding mine.

Daddy and the River

Daddy was washing his car by the river,
shirt off, humming an old *harana* [32],
sunlight glinting off the chrome and his sweat—
a quiet man in a loud world.

Then—*bang!*
A sound too sharp to belong to nature,
to belong to peace.
The water shivered,
and he fell to his knees,
hand pressed to his side,
eyes wide but steady.

A few corrupt men,
faces hidden by the blur of uniform and power,
had made him a target that day.
No reason. No warning.
Just the cruel echo of control.

But Daddy—
Daddy stood.
He walked.

---

[32] A romantic serenade

Step by step down that dirt road to town,

his blood darkening the dust.

Mama held my hand,

both of us trembling in the *jeepney* [33]

that rattled like it might fall apart.

I remember her voice—half prayer, half command—

as we bounced from one hospital to another,

the night dragging its feet behind us.

My grandfather lived.

By some stubborn mercy, he lived.

And now, whenever I hear river water rushing,

I see him there again—

steady, wounded, unbroken—

washing his car as if nothing had changed,

as if courage were just

another chore to finish before sundown.

---

[33] Jeeps used as public transportation

Cool Like That

Back then, I thought divorce was an American thing—
like Pop-Tarts,
or Saturday morning cartoons,
or having your own room with posters on the wall.

My friends would say,
"I'm going to my dad's this weekend,"
and it sounded so casual,
so free—
like they got to live two lives,
two houses,
two Christmases.

I'd go home to Mama and Papa
still arguing in Ilonggo whispers
behind the thin walls,
and I'd wonder
why we couldn't be more like them—
the Americans,
who got to split their lives in half
and still somehow be whole.

In the Philippines,
divorce wasn't just rare—

it was unthinkable.
You stayed.
You prayed.
You swallowed your unhappiness
and called it faith.

But in my child mind,
I saw something shiny in the cracks—
my friends' divorced parents
with new cars, new partners,
new lives that looked like choices.
And I wanted that.
I wanted us to be cool like that—
modern, brave,
a little broken,
but *American.*

Now I see it different—
how staying and leaving
both carry their own kind of courage,
how love and resentment
can live in the same room,
and how a child's version of "cool"
was really just
the wish for something quieter,

something softer

than the sound of parents

pretending to still belong

to each other.

Chicharon Bulaklak

I remember the day Tita Letty fried *chicharon bulaklak* [34]—
the kitchen already thick with anticipation,
her hands moving like magic over the bubbling oil.

And then—*pop! sizzle!*—
grease leapt from the pan like fireworks,
smearing the walls, the counters,
even the ceiling, I think,
while we ducked and laughed.

The air smelled like pork and fire,
hot and sweet and impossible to ignore.
And when we finally tasted it—
crispy, golden, tender in ways the eye couldn't predict—
all the mess, all the chaos,
felt like the point of it all.

I left the kitchen with stains on my shirt,
smile stuck to my face,
knowing some memories are made
from grease, laughter,
and something so good it burns a little.

---

[34] A popular street food of fried pork mesentery

Weslaco

When I moved to Texas,

the sky felt too wide,

the nights too quiet

without Mama's voice or Papa's laughter.

The air smelled of dust and something new—

like the world was still deciding

if I belonged.

Then came my cousins—

a burst of noise and warmth,

bare feet on tile, laughter spilling down hallways.

Joy took my hand

like she had been saving it all this time.

She became the sister I never had,

sharing her jeans and

sharing secrets beneath the whirl of ceiling fans.

And the boys—five of them—

rough, loud, teasing,

each one claiming me in their own way:

with jokes, with nicknames,

with the kind of love that bumps your shoulder

instead of saying *"I missed you."*

In that crowded house,

I learned the sound of belonging again—

not from blood alone,

but from shared meals,

borrowed clothes,

late-night laughter echoing into the Texas dark.

I had left my parents,

but somehow gained a family twice over—

one that taught me

home isn't always where you start,

but where someone waits

with open arms and a plate of rice.

Spectator

I was three—
bare feet on the table,
crusts of *pan de sal* [35] beside me,
the air thick with laundry steam
and gossip turned to thunder.

Two maids—our maids—
hair tangled like fishing nets,
voices cracking in Ilonggo,
the kind of words Nanay
would've washed my mouth for.

A slipper flew.
A rosary swung from the wall.
I just sat there—
small as a teacup,
wide-eyed,
legs swinging in time
with the shouting.

Then Tita Eva bursts in,
the way a storm enters a quiet noon.
"Why didn't you get someone?" she gasped,

---

[35] A staple yeasty bread roll in the Philippines, usually dunked in coffee

and I, without shame or fear,

said, *"It was fun to watch."*

And oh—

the way her hand covered her mouth,

half gasp, half laugh—

that was the day I learned

grown-up chaos

could be its own kind of cartoon,

and that sometimes,

even grown-ups

didn't always know

how to be big.

The Bells of Capistrano

I was small, shoes scuffing
the sun-warmed stones of Mission San Juan,
the bells tolling like whispered histories,
each clang a story I half-understood.

White stucco walls, red-tiled roofs,
arched corridors where shadows played
and courtyard fountains murmured
in a language older than my tongue.

I felt it there—the Spanish touch—
the swirl of faith and adobe,
the way the air smelled of citrus and dust,
like afternoons in my hometown.

I thought of the Philippines,
of me tracing my fingers
over carved wooden doors,
of churches with bell towers rising
like miniature mountains,
of priests in cassocks and pressed robes
singing to God beneath painted ceilings.

Here, it was the same and not the same—
a strange reflection of home,
echoes of a distant island
woven into the hills of California.

I ran along the cloister,
my shadow chasing my small feet,
wondering how the ocean carried memory
from one shore to another,
how a child could recognize
the heartbeat of home
in a land so far away.

Setter

I was always the one beneath the ball,
hands open, waiting,
the world slowing just enough
for me to decide where it should go.

Setter—
the invisible position,
not the one who spikes,
but the one who makes the spike possible.
Precision was my language,
control my heartbeat.
Every toss, a chance to prove
I belonged.

I dove across gym floors
burnished with sweat and echo,
kneepads torn,
palms stinging from the slap of the ball.
Every point was a heartbeat,
every serve, a test.

The crowd never chanted my name,
but I didn't need them to.
I needed the perfect arc—

the ball floating up

like something holy,

landing in waiting hands,

and then the *slap*—

proof that my unseen work mattered.

Maybe I wasn't just setting volleyballs.

Maybe I was setting myself—

into this new country,

into classrooms where my accent felt too loud,

into the rhythm of fitting in.

Every match was a declaration:

I can make something out of nothing.

I can take what's thrown my way

and make it rise.

Even now,

when life sends its wild serves,

I still lift my hands—

steady, ready,

remembering that girl

who found belonging

in the brief, perfect flight

of a ball.

Pandanggo Dreams

Spotlight hits.

My feet—bare, trembling—kiss the wooden stage.

Music rolls in,
a river of strings from the *rondalla* [36],
and suddenly I am both the dancer
and the fire I hold.

Candles balanced on my hands and head,
tiny flames like stubborn little hearts
refusing to flicker out.

I see the rhythm
that pulses through my veins,
that whispers my Nanay's stories,
my Mama's laughter,
my own heartbeat.

I pivot, sway, step,
and the candles swing with me—
tiny suns floating in the dark,

---

[36] A string ensemble

casting shadows that stretch

like the dreams I carried in my backpack.

I feel the stage beneath me,

the weight of tradition,

the sparkle of every eye,

and for a moment—

I am infinite.

I am light.

I am *Pandanggo sa Ilaw* [37].

---

[37] A Filipino folk dance known as the "Dance of Light," in which the dancer balances three oil lamps on their hands and head

Miss Kinder and the Cassava Curls

All my life,
my hair was Asian poker straight—
the kind that defied gravity, humidity,
and every curling iron in town.
It hung like a well-behaved child:
quiet, obedient,
never one to cause drama.

But the year I became *Miss Kinder,*
float, gown, and all,
I wanted to be fabulous.
I wanted curls—
big, bouncy, beauty-queen curls
that said *Miss Universe.*

Mama and Tita Judith looked at each other
like two scientists about to break a sacred law.
No curlers?
No problem.
They went out back
and harvested twigs from the cassava tree,
snapping them like destiny itself.
"We'll make it work," Tita said,

as if we were launching a space shuttle

instead of a four-year-old's hairdo.

They twisted and wrapped every strand,

tied with rubber bands,

spritzed with cologne water for luck.

I slept that night

feeling like a porcupine in a tiara.

By morning—

oh, the miracle.

My hair had volume,

if not direction.

A poufy cloud of defiance,

each curl pointing to a different province.

Mama gasped.

Tita clapped.

I twirled in my itchy gown,

glitter falling like confetti

from some unseen celebration.

And as I rode that float,

smiling like a queen

with the confidence of a thousand cassava sticks,

I thought,

Maybe beauty is just ambition with bad aim.

Because my curls were a mess—
but for one glorious day,
my hair wasn't straight.
And that was enough.

Tita Ems and Me

She wasn't blood,
but she was family—
Tita Ems, Papa's school teacher,
with her quick laugh
and stories that smelled of salt air
and afternoons spent wandering.

She slept on a board,
her posture the straightest I'd ever seen,
a spine like a ruler,
her independence shining in every movement.
Her English grammar was impeccable;
she corrected me constantly,
sharp, full of life,
never letting small mistakes slide.

I became her companion,
her shadow in sun and sand,
riding with her to Balboa Island,
windows down,
AM radio crackling
with the ghosts of 1940s songs—
crooners and brass,

and the world spinning slower
just for us.

We ate at Chinese restaurants
like we owned them,
always asking for crispy noodles
that crackled under chopsticks,
drizzled with hot mustard
and sweet and sour sauce,
our fingers sticky,
our laughter louder than the clatter of plates.

She was the one who made ordinary streets
feel like oceans of possibility.
She taught me how to float in a boat,
how to savor every bite,
how to hear music
and feel it spin around the corners of your heart.

Tita Ems and I—
we collected moments, not things,
songs in our heads,
and the quiet understanding
that family
is sometimes chosen,

and sometimes

the most unforgettable of all.

Durian Fields

The air was thick—
sweet, strange, and sharp enough
to stop you mid-breath.
That was the smell of durian fields
ripening under the sun,
where green husks split like secrets,
and the earth itself seemed to sigh.

Some called it rotten,
some called it heaven—
but to me,
it was home.
That wild perfume rising from the soil,
a mix of fruit and rain and memory.
Flies hummed around fallen ones,
the trees heavy with golden bombs of scent,
and somewhere,
someone always laughed,
"Who could love a smell like that?"

But I did.
Because that smell meant mornings
with barefoot cousins and sticky fingers,
meat soft as butter,

stories rolling as easy as the breeze.

Even now, oceans away,
one whiff of something ripe and forbidden
and I'm back there—
under the canopy of thorned fruit,
breathing in the heart of the motherland,
where love was never delicate,
but always strong enough
to linger.

Carabao

There was a time the world felt slower—

when afternoons stretched long

and the river held its own kind of silence.

That's where he stood—

the water carabao.

Half submerged,

half myth.

He didn't move much.

He just was—

the color of the earth itself,

breathing with the same rhythm

as the land that raised us.

We used to walk down there—

barefoot, unhurried,

the air thick with sunlight and gossip,

the kind of heat that softened everything—

skin, memory, pride.

He'd turn his head,

just enough to see us,

then look away.

A gesture that said:

"I've seen generations come and go.

You're just passing through."

Thrifted Dreams in Tustin

Mama and I wandered Tustin streets,
thrift store windows lining our small adventure,
searching for a dress
while other girls counted mall bags and new heels.

Racks of polyester and faded florals
brushed against our fingertips.
I tried on too-big jackets,
too-short skirts,
each one a quiet reminder
that money didn't bend for us.

But Mama's eyes kept looking,
steady and warm,
until a black velvet shimmer caught the light—
strappy, simple, perfect.
I held it against my chest,
and she smiled,
knowing we had found something more than fabric.

At graduation, I wore it like armor,
like hope stitched into every seam,
while classmates twirled in new labels.
And Mama clapped the loudest,

her hands soft but proud,

because we had found magic

between thrifted racks and love.

Echoes of Papa

I was fifteen—
the world tipped over,
spilled like a glass I couldn't catch.

Papa's laugh—
bright corners of our house—
gone.

I searched for it
in the kitchen where he cooked *Kinilaw* [38],
in the car where he drove us around,
his voice threading stories between turns.

I remember him bald from the chemo—
the Filipino Mr. Clean—
and I laughed through the ache,
because he could still make the world lighter.

I miss his sternness,
how it held me straight,
and his forgiveness,
soft as the air after rain.

---

[38] A dish of raw seafood cooked in vinegar and citrus juices

At his funeral,

jasmine, lilies,

the air thick with what I couldn't hold,

and somewhere,

the song *"Oh My Papa"*

flickered through the silence,

soft, trembling,

wrapping around my chest like a hand

I would never hold again.

He lies forever in California,

and I—

I'm a world away in North Carolina,

reaching,

and the air answers

with the faintest echo of his voice.

Ili-Ili

Mama's voice was soft as dusk,
threading through the slats of our window
where the air smelled of rice and rain.
Every night, she sang:
Ili-ili tulog anay [39],
but she changed the words—
not *your Nanay's out to buy some bread,*
but *your Tatay's out to buy some bread.*

I didn't know who that was,
this Papa *(Tatay)* who lived inside her song.
He was a ghost that sent boxes—
with shoes too big,
shirts that smelled faintly of cologne and distance,
and chocolate that melted
before it reached the table.

Mama said he worked hard,
that one day we'd join him.
But I only knew him
through her eyes—
the way they softened

---

[39] *Hush, hush go to sleep.*

when she sang,

the way her voice trembled

on his name.

So I'd close mine,

pretend the creak of the ceiling fan

was the ocean between us,

pretend his footsteps

echoed in the hallway,

pretend his bread

was almost ready to come home.

Years later,

when I finally met him—

real skin, real voice,

no longer just a promise in a parcel—

I realized how deep a lullaby can reach,

how it can hold a whole family

in one trembling note.

And now that he's gone,

I still find myself listening at night,

half expecting the door to open,

the smell of bread in the air,

as if he's just running late again—

as if Papa's still out there,

somewhere past the sea,
buying bread.

Blue Grand Am

It was Papa's car—
the blue Pontiac Grand Am,
color chosen by my brother
because the Blue Power Ranger was his favorite,
still humming his songs through the speakers
like they were written just for him.

When he passed,
the keys felt too heavy in my hand—
like inheritance and goodbye
had merged into one small piece of metal.
I drove it everywhere,
windows down,
pretending he was riding shotgun,
hand tapping the rhythm on the dash.

That night on the 5 South,
Santa Ana lights blurring into streaks,
the world came apart in metal and glass.
Brakes screaming.
Headlights folding into each other.
My heart stopped long enough
to make space for his name.

When the dust settled,

my car—his car—

was crushed like a tin offering.

And I—

not even a scratch.

Not even a bruise.

The air smelled of jasmine and lilies—

the same flowers from his funeral,

ghosting through the chaos,

soft and impossible.

I knew then

he was there.

Not in the wreckage,

but in the mercy that wrapped itself around me.

Sometimes I still dream of that night—

the sound of twisting steel,

the light too bright to look at.

But mostly I remember

the scent of flowers in the air,

and the strange peace that whispered,

"Not yet, Inday."

Papa's car was gone,

but he stayed.

Just long enough
to steer me back
into the living.

Cat's in the Cradle

Papa loved that song—
Cat's in the Cradle by Harry Chapin.
He'd hum along in the car,
hand drumming the steering wheel,
his voice low and certain
on the line about the boy
growing up just like him.

Back then, I didn't understand.
I was too small,
too busy counting the power lines
as they flew past the window.
But now, when that song plays,
I can't breathe right for a moment.

Because he never got to see it—
my brother and I,
grown, busy,
too busy,
just like in the song.
He never saw us juggling our days,
our kids calling for us
the way we used to call for him.

Sometimes I wonder if he knew,

if somewhere deep down

he sang that song as a prayer

or a warning.

If he sensed

he'd miss the part

where the boy becomes the man,

and the man becomes the memory.

Now, when I hear that melody—

that soft ache of guitar and truth—

I imagine him somewhere,

tapping the rhythm on the dashboard of forever,

smiling that quiet, knowing smile.

And I whisper along,

"Yeah, Papa,

I finally get it now."

Tubig sa Bukid

Mountain Water

When my skin burned and itched raw,
Daddy climbed the rocks barefoot,
a glass bottle glinting in his hand,
to fetch water from the sulfur spring.

The air smelled like eggs and earth,
steam rising like ghosts from the stones.
He said the mountain's sulfur water could heal,
and I believed him—
because his love always carried truth.

He poured it gently over my arms,
cool first, then warm, then sting—
but his touch was steady as prayer.

That day, I watched his back grow small
against the mountain light,
and I understood without words
that this was how he said *Palangga taka* [40]—
one climb, one glass bottle at a time.

---

[40] *I love you.*

Mouthing the Words

Cap and gown.
Choir robes.
Flag hanging high.

We line up shoulder to shoulder,
hands over hearts,
the music teacher nods—
and we sing.

"I'm proud to be an American…"

And my voice—
it cracks.
Not because I forgot the words—
but because they didn't belong to me.

I wasn't an American.
Not then.
Maybe not ever.

Still, I sang like I could earn it.
Like every note was an application,
every harmony a plea.

I made Honor Roll.

Got straight A's.

Spoke perfect English.

Smiled the right way.

Stood up for the pledge.

Stood still when they said *freedom*.

But inside—

inside I knew—

there are papers that speak louder than dreams,

laws that don't bend for good intentions,

walls you can't climb

no matter how high your grades go.

Still, I sang.

Because maybe—

just maybe—

belonging starts

before the paperwork.

Because maybe love for a country

isn't stamped or sealed.

It's something you carry in your chest,

even when it doesn't carry you back.

So yes—

I sang *"I'm proud to be an American,"*

choking on every word,

hoping one day

the country I loved so much

would finally sing back to me.

Two Shores, One Ocean

I'm in Newport Beach
where Maseratis hum past million-dollar homes
and surfers carve the waves like artists
while I'm just chasing clam chowder
in a Styrofoam bowl on the pier, steam curling up to my face.

A few thousand miles away,
my old beaches in the Philippines
smell of fish and salt and coconut husks,
fishermen hauling nets
while children chase crabs across fine sand.

Same Pacific Ocean,
different rhythms, different lives—
one shore polished, shining, glossy
the other raw, alive, untamed.

I hold my bowl tight,
taste the ocean in every spoonful,
and wonder if somewhere across the water
a child is doing the same thing,
just with a net instead of a surfboard.

But for a moment—

just a taste —

the pier became

a bridge.

A bridge between worlds.

Two shores, one ocean,

and somehow, for a moment,

I belong to both.

Home, Again

I step off the small plane
and the streets of Bacolod City feel too wide,
the signs too sharp,
my tongue stumbling
over words I used to own.

Faces smile,
but they look past me,
like I'm a shadow
of the child who left.

Then—
the market hits me first.
Mangoes like sun in my hands,
ginamos tingling my nose,
the steam of *adobo*[41] curling up
and suddenly—
my mouth remembers
what my brain forgot.

I run to the waterfall,
water slapping my skin,
cold and alive,

---

[41] A traditional chicken dish with a vinegar base and spices

like the country itself
is shaking the years off me.

Nanay grabs me,
her arms a harbor,
Daddy laughs,
his voice a drum
beating the rhythm I've missed.

And in the taste,
in the water,
in the hug—
I am home.

Not the streets,
not the language,
not the years away—
just this:
heartbeat, laughter, salt, spice, sun,
and the ocean whispering
that I have always belonged.

Here, language is secondary.
Here, the heart remembers
even when the mind forgets.

And somewhere nearby,

a *Sampaguita* [42] blooms—

pure, simple, devoted—

its small white petals

promising that home

was never lost,

only waiting.

---

[42] The national flower of the Philippines that signifies a promise, dignity and beauty. Sweet-smelling and pure, it translates to "I promise you."

www.ingramcontent.com/pod-product-compliance
Lightning Source LLC
Chambersburg PA
CBHW020356130626
46549CB00006B/2301